NATIONAL
GEOGRAPHIC

School Publishing

Jobs

Rowan Sellers

PICTURE CREDITS

Illustrations by David Legge (4–5, 14–15).

Cover, 1, 2, 6 (all), 7 (right), 8 (right), 9 (all), 10 (below right), 12 (all), 13 (all), 16 (all except bottom), Photolibrary.com; 7 (left), 11 (below right), 16 (bottom), APL/Corbis; 8 (left), Jeff Greenberg/PhotoEdit, Inc.; 10 (above left), Getty Images; 11 (above left), APL.

Produced through the worldwide resources of the National Geographic Society, John M. Fahey, Jr., President and Chief Executive Officer; Gilbert M. Grosvenor, Chairman of the Board; Nina D. Hoffman, Executive Vice President and President, Books and Education Publishing Group.

PREPARED BY NATIONAL GEOGRAPHIC SCHOOL PUBLISHING

Ericka Markman, Senior Vice President and President Children's Books and Education Publishing Group; Steve Mico, Senior Vice President and Publisher; Marianne Hiland, Editorial Director; Lynnette Brent, Executive Editor; Michael Murphy and Barbara Wood, Senior Editors; Bea Jackson, Design Director; David Dumo, Art Director; Margaret Sidlowsky, Illustrations Director; Matt Wascavage, Manager of Publishing Services; Sean Philpotts, Production Manager.

MANUFACTURING AND QUALITY MANAGEMENT

Christopher A. Liedel, Chief Financial Officer; Phillip L. Schlosser, Director; Clifton M. Brown III, Manager.

BOOK DEVELOPMENT

Ibis for Kids Australia Pty Limited.

Published by the National Geographic Society
1145 17th Street, N.W.
Washington, D.C. 20036-4688

ISBN: 0-7922-6057-0

Fifth Printing June 2018
Printed in the USA

Contents

Find people who are working.
Tell about their jobs.

Health

Some people help us stay healthy.

doctor

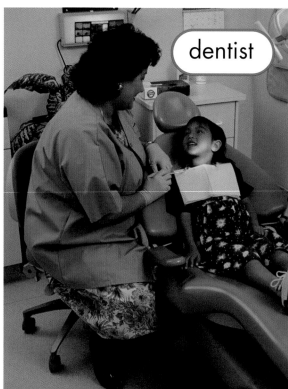

dentist

Safety

Some people help us stay safe.

police officer

fire fighter

Learning

Some people help us learn.

park ranger

teacher

Slates
Listen
Think
Write
Show
Clear

hide and seek
board
trains
Let's Play
games
ball
kating
de bike
rollerblade
jump rope

Making

Some people make things we need.

baker

shoemaker

Selling

Some people sell things we need.

clothing salesperson

grocery clerk

Building

Some people build things we need.

house builders

bridge builders

Other Jobs

People do many other jobs, too.
Can you think of more jobs?

car mechanic

plumber

musician

cooks

farmer

13

What work are these people doing?
What job would you like to do?

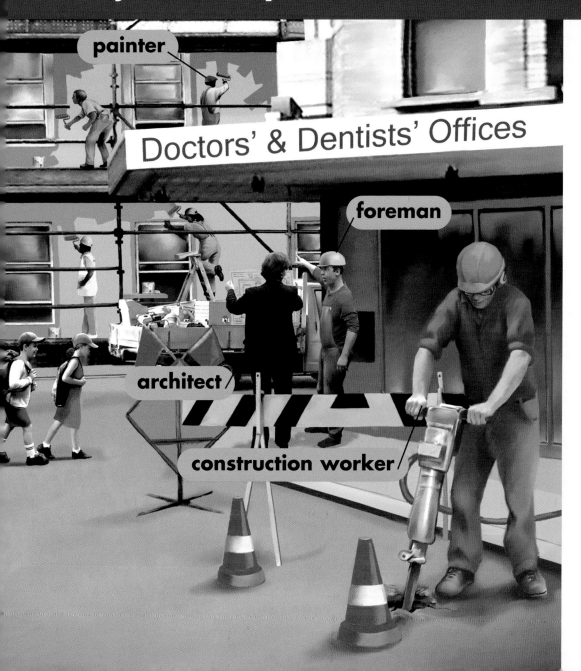

help

job

people

work

worker

Picture Index